LITTLE IDEAS, BIG BUSINESS

5 STEPS

TO TURN

your ideas

INTO A

Business

BILLY MCLEAN

Copyright © 2021

Published by Belinda McLean, Melbourne Australia

All rights reserved. No part of this publication may be reproduced, distributed or transmitted in any form or by any means, without prior written permission.

Book Layout © 2021

Little Ideas, Big Business: 5 Steps to Turn your Ideas into a Business

ISBN 978-0-6450554-4-3

Your ideas are as unique as your fingerprints

— BILLY MCLEAN

Introduction

It's not that I couldn't work my corporate job, it's that I didn't want to anymore.

I was told that if I studied hard, got good grades, was a good girl and put in the time, I would be rewarded. Promotions, responsibility, financial freedom.

When the time came to have a family, I was also told I could fit that into my career as well.

I was told that I could have it all. And I believed them.

As I caught two trains and a bus home and then fought traffic five days a week; stressed, frustrated and exhausted. I realized… I can't have it all. Not like this anyway.

It was a sudden and profound realization. That this wasn't the way I wanted to live. Going round in circles trying to please everyone and ruining my own sanity in the process. There had to be a better way. The problem was… I had never met anyone who showed me any other alternative.

I thought that the choice was a career or a mum. That was it. It wasn't until I met a brilliant coach who was doing things differently that I realized there were so many more options available. My eyes were opened up to the possibilities and the ideas started to flow.

And flowed and flowed. Until I had a flood of ideas and was stuck in the overwhelm of what to work on next.

That's when the light bulb went on. My career wasn't wasted at all. I could use all the skills I'd acquired in my career and direct them to a more entrepreneurial business. One that I owned. One that served me and my family. Not the other way around.

This book shares the simple formula that helped me go from a bucket full of ideas (none of which I executed) to a thriving business that fits around me and my family. My engineer brain, it turns out, is quite helpful for other mums, other entrepreneurs, and anyone that wants to go from ideas, to execution. From chaos to focus. From a career that overwhelms you, to a business that fulfills.

Acknowledgements

To my husband, Mike, who reminds me to keep things in perspective, yet supports my wild dreams; love you & thank you. Thanks for being a sounding board, picking up the slack and saying it (whatever it was!) as I needed to hear it.

To my girls, Becky & Lucy; love you both! You might not get how much your questions & support mean quite yet, but know I cherish them!

To all those who have supported me to get this book finished (you know who you are!); it sounds cliché, but it wouldn't be done if not for your encouraging, blunt, kind & celebratory words. What a blessing to know you all!

To the reader; if you only get this far in the book... know that your ideas, dreams and goals matter! I hope this sparks you to remember that you are able to follow your unique path and celebrate as you go!

About the Author

Billy McLean is an Aussie mum, author, coach and entrepreneur.

Billy is a solar power engineer & spent much of her time training & travelling. Though Billy loved the work she did in her chosen field, it took her away from being the wife, mother & change-agent that she saw herself to be.

The frustration of working to someone else's plan & timeline stifled her creativity and entrepreneurial spirit. After working in many industries, including as an employee, network marketer and contractor, she realised the common theme of her frustration and restlessness was that the frameworks were not her own. She wanted to unleash her gifts & purpose by creating her own business that she could thrive in; so she became an entrepreneur.

Now she runs her own coaching & consultancy business from her home in Victoria, helping women create home-based businesses with purpose. With clients all over the world, she is building a community of women who are turning their little ideas into big business around their family.

Billy is an advocate for boldly declaring those pie-in-the-sky dreams we all have and pulling out the stops in pursuit of flipping those ideas into action. All of this in the name of letting your skills & value shine.

Billy loves connecting with nature through gardening, bushwalking and camping, and finds these passions refreshing & calming in the midst of the constant busyness of modern life. She advocates time out in nature to slow down and channel all those creative ideas that come when you give them time & space.

Her ultimate goal is to get women reinvigorated; about their choices, their potential and their purpose. She sets women on a journey to rediscover their inspiration & ultimately follow their unique path.

CONTENTS

- A Career & a Family 1
- The 3 Desires of the New Workforce 7
  - Flexibility 7
  - Money 10
  - Purpose: Doing Work you Love 11
  - There are Roadblocks, you can Overcome them 12
  - What am I going to Sell? 15
  - From Prototype to Production 18
  - If you don't Overcome Roadblocks 20
  - If you don't get Prototype to Production right .. 22
- Overcoming Roadblocks 23
  - The Capability Roadblock 24
  - The Perfectionism Roadblock 24
  - The Time Roadblock 26
  - Fear of Success or Fear of Failure? 27
  - Overcoming Self-Sabotage 28
  - Removing Roadblocks From the Past 31
  - Releasing Perfectionism 34
  - Valuing Your Ideas 37
  - Hobbies vs. Business 38
  - Undervaluing Ourselves 39
  - Do you Give Away Free Stuff? 47
  - Decision Time 50

The 5 Steps 51
  Turning Your Ideas into a Business 51
  Step 1: The Brain Dump 53
  Your Product Solar System 57
  Step 2: Figure Out & Focus on One Idea 59
  Money Now vs Half-Baked vs Concept Ideas 60
  Money Now Ideas 60
  Half-Baked Ideas 62
  Concept Ideas 63
  Step 3: Putting in Celebration Dates (Deadlines) 64
  Step 4: The Minimum Viable Product 68
  Step 5: Prioritise Your Actions 72
  Necessities, Niceties & Bonuses 73
  Series & Parallel Actions 76
  A Note on Distractions 79
  Procrastination Habits 80
Prototype to Production 81
  The top 10 causes of small business failure 83
  Reflecting on Where You are Right Now 84
  Version 2.0 & Beyond 86
  Scaling the Business 88
It's Your Turn 91

Chapter One

A Career & a Family

My training as an engineer taught me so many things... But it didn't teach me how to how to have a career & a family at the same time.

I was an engineer with a successful career in solar, working long hours until we decided to have kids (it is never 9.00am – 5.00pm, it is more like 7.30am – 6.00pm with the commute... you know the deal, right?). I wanted to be at home with my kids and not working like those kinds of hours; so when we had our first child, I quit.

I grew up in a generation that was told they could have it all. They were wrong.

All my life I'd been given well-meaning advice. Study hard, get a good job, with a reputable company, put in the hours, build a solid future for yourself, and eventually you'll be rewarded. But the future I was looking at didn't interest me anymore. I couldn't reconcile the demands of work and my desire to be a fully engaged mum.

I was at peace with that; but also knew I didn't want to only be a stay at home Mum. I knew I would go back to some sort of work eventually. I was content with being at home with the kids when they were young, and was happy and excited I could be there with them for those times.

When they started school and their reliance on me changed (some say 'dwindled', but really, as mums we know it just changes!), I wanted to fill that extra time with some type of work. I tried a few things, but was never really 100% passionate about any of them. I would experiment with something for six months to a year, but the fire would die out & I would get restless. Then my attention would shift to something new, something to ignite the passion again.

I wanted to earn some money and contribute to the household budget, but more importantly, to do work which was fun, engaging and challenging. That didn't seem available to me in traditional jobs. Working for someone else and needing flexibility, because you are a Mum, meant I couldn't deep dive into the projects I was passionate about, so (if I'm being really honest!) I got bored & disheartened quickly. It felt like if I wanted a job with responsibility that was challenging and engaging, I had to sacrifice time with my family. Talking to other mums it seems that this was a shared experience for so many people.

Even when I was looking at job advertisements; I felt I could do the work, but I just couldn't 100% commit to someone else's dream. It was not where my heart was and I didn't want to be stuck for a long time in a job I didn't enjoy. I've met so many people who don't enjoy their work and that breaks my heart. So much of our time is spent at work; it's soul-destroying to see people keep doing a job they hate year in, year out.

I was at a fork in the road: one path felt like being put in a box, mundane and not fulfilling; the other was covered in fog. There was no direction or path, I just felt there must be something else for me.

I realized, while I was applying for jobs and doing little bits and pieces, I had so many ideas and so much more to give than that. Why couldn't I DO my ideas? Why couldn't I do what I loved doing? Why couldn't I help others and, in the process, get paid for it?

What I hadn't understood was that my training as an engineer would give me a framework to build a new career around, one that I was in control of. One that was infinitely more satisfying, more rewarding and gave me the freedom to be a mum and a business

I was at a fork in the road.

One path felt mundane.

The other was covered in fog.

woman. But how do I make that happen? How do I bring my ideas to life?

Then I met a coach who said OF COURSE I could do all of that. You can do what you love, help others AND bring in a very decent income! It was like I needed to be given permission by someone else, and once that happened, I could run with it! It seems silly, hey? I knew I *could* do it, but when someone else said it, I got the *confidence* to do it.

I now knew there was a path, but I was still unclear how to get to the destination; I just needed to figure out the steps to get from A to B. The steps that would take me towards my ultimate goal and the bright future I saw for both myself and my clients.

Today I run a training and coaching business with in person coaching programs and a range of online products designed to help other mums who found themselves in the same situation I did; lots of ideas, but stuck in a merry-go-round of what if's and roadblocks. I serve clients from all over the globe and use all kinds of technology that enables me to work from wherever I am, even if that's in my garden.

My experience is that many other women, and an increasing number of men, are looking for greater flexibility in their time. It seems that the freedom to use your time how you wish is fast becoming the most valuable currency of all. Close behind that is to find more meaning in our work while at the same time taking advantage of a global entrepreneurial economy to increase our incomes.

This book is a practical guide to how you too can take a different path and find a better balance in your life. How you can take your ideas and put them into action.

We'll help you know how to overcome many of the common roadblocks, and give you the simple secrets that engineers are taught to take ideas and get them into action.

Chapter Two

The 3 Desires of the New Workforce

I believe there are three key desires of the general workforce at the moment; flexibility, purpose and money. If you ask people about what they'd like to change in their job, it generally falls under these three categories. Let's explore that a bit further.

Flexibility

Everyone's priorities are different; so it's all about the flexibility to choose. Not many people in day jobs get to do that. In a "job" you are told you have to physically be there, you get paid this much, and that's it. If you don't want to be there that day, or if you want to get paid more this month, that's quite often not in your power to change.

When you realise you can have the flexibility to work more this month because you need the extra cash, or you will work less and spend more time with your family because that's what you need right now, it is an attractive path. That flexibility is taken away in a 9 to 5 job.

When you have this structure in place, and you've properly gone through the steps; you get to a point where you have the ability and confidence to say 'yes' or 'no'.

When you have that flexibility, you can be more generous. You can decide to give a little extra time or money, or a combination. For many people that option is simply not available; they just physically can't.

There are also positive health benefits to enjoying your work and knowing you're helping people. Imagine how different your day would feel if when you get up, and you think, "Woohoo! I'm going to work!" rather than, "Well, I better get ready to get on the train, again. I guess I better suit up for tackle the day…"

When you have Flexibility, you can be more Generous.

Money

Right up front: money DOES matter. Period. This doesn't mean you're a greedy Scrooge because you want to actually make a profit on what you do.

If you are going to have a business, not a hobby, but a business, you need to be producing money. It needs to be financially good in terms of time versus money because if it isn't, it costs you & becomes a huge stress.

In a 2014 study in the UK; 62% said money was one of the biggest stressors in their relationships; almost double that of infidelity (36%) [A1]. If money is a stressor, it impacts all areas of our lives; from our business to our relationships, how we live & where we live. I'm not saying we have to be zillionaires but having financial freedom and bringing that income in is important.

[A1] https://www.dailymail.co.uk/news/article-2950658/Money-worries-bigger-strain-relationships-AFFAIR-according-study-nation-s-happiness.html

Secondly, money is a tool; something to be used. Money in itself is not good or bad; righteous or evil. It just is. However, money amplifies parts of our personality. If you have more money, you can be more generous, but you can also be greedier. Having money available to you means you can invest in the areas most important to you.

Both flexibility and money give you options. If you want to be with your kids on their special days, like school sports or awards, or birthdays, you can take those off without having to ask. If you have enough finances; you can say 'no' to inconvenient or untimely jobs; even if someone is offering twice your rate, but it's your daughter's birthday… you have the option to say 'no thanks'.

Having your finances in order means you can confidently say no when you'd like & not stress about it at all. The choice is *actually* yours.

In 2015-2017, Mental Health America surveyed over 17,000 employees about their workplace satisfaction. Over 80% of respondents said that "The stress from my job affects my relationships with my family or friends". And 63% of people agreed that "The frustration or stress from my job causes me to engage in unhealthy behaviours, such as drinking or crying regularly" [*A2].

That's over 10,000 people by the way! This is not the way we were designed to spend so many years of our lives!

[*A2] https://www.mhanational.org/sites/default/files/Mind%20the%20Workplace%20-%20MHA%20Workplace%20Health%20Survey%202017%20FINAL.PDF

Purpose: Doing Work you Love

Many people are unsatisfied in their jobs because they feel no connection to where the company is going or what it is doing; it is just a J.O.B. In the book *Rich Dad, Poor Dad*, Robert T. Kiyosaki wrote "Job is an acronym for 'Just Over Broke.".. Hmmm… so you are doing work that causes issues with your loved ones, issues with your health (mental & physical) and you're barely making ends meet?

The psychological benefits to being connected to a purpose are huge. What it means for most people on a day to day basis is they feel happier, have more energy, and can give more of that to their families and people they love. They get excited, not just about things like birthday parties, but to see their clients because they know they are doing good things, and that brings a smile to their faces every day.

So this is the flipside to working a J.O.B.: you CAN be doing stuff that you enjoy and get paid for it. You CAN wake up excited for life… for "work"; if you even call it that now, because you enjoy it so much! You CAN be part of a team that you get a positive buzz from and enjoy being around. AND (added bonus!): if you are in a community connected to a higher purpose, studies show you will live a longer and happier life. [*A3]

[*A3] https://pubmed.ncbi.nlm.nih.gov/31451635/

There are Roadblocks, you can Overcome them

If there were not any roadblocks to creating this type of business, you would already be doing it, right? We need to look at why we haven't done it already and acknowledge that so we can move forward. These are Roadblocks.

LITTLE IDEAS, BIG BUSINESS • 13

J.O.B
Just Over Broke

- Robert Kiyosaki

Imagine you stubbed your toe getting out of bed, and you're frustrated. Then something else happens like you spill your coffee. How much more frustrated are you because you were already frustrated? If you focus on the annoyance and frustration, then it's super hard to move forward; and likely when you talk to someone; the first thing you are going to mention is your sore toe & your stained shirt.

If you stubbed your toe while you were helping a friend move or grabbing something for a client from the shelf; you're unlikely to dwell on it as much as you have something bigger you are doing. You may say "ouch!" and mention it in passing, but quickly you keep moving on as there are others waiting for you.

You're working towards something outside yourself. That roadblock becomes small, and you can move forward quickly.

When I was a child, I was noted to be intelligent, but for a long time I didn't tell people because I was embarrassed. Teachers told me not to answer so many questions so other children could have a turn. But what that actually taught me was I shouldn't speak or put myself out there because I will be told to be quiet. But I also got really disappointed when I didn't get what I was aiming for or achieve what I wanted because I didn't speak up.

This was one of my big Roadblocks. Maybe you know some of yours already? (No stress if you don't; we'll work through them when they come up!)

I worked through this roadblock using Aroma Freedom Technique (AFT) for my deep-rooted belief I needed to stay quiet and I had an ugly voice. Sound strange, that I would carry that thought around for years & years? Sometimes these roadblocks seem a little quirky, but trust me: give them the time & space they need to be acknowledged so you can move forward.

Once you identify & work through them, they don't magically disappear overnight, but through AFT, you have a method and game plan of what to do when they do reappear (& you'll be able to identify them so much more easily; no more being blind-sided!)

I would have likely written this book years ago if I had figured out that roadblock! I know I have an amazing mind and amazing ideas and I need to share them with others, because it is selfish not to share when you've got a good thing happening, right? (Remember that; you have amazing ideas too!)

What am I going to Sell?

Sometimes we get overwhelmed with all of the business options available to us. We could do workshops, courses, write a book, or any number of other beautiful ideas... but nothing gets finished to the point we can actually put it out into the world.

We will go through The Five Steps to take all of those ideas in your head so you don't lose them, and get to a point where you can actually put something valuable out there that you will get paid for and get satisfaction out of.

A lot of people spend time doing bits and pieces but never actually finish one product to put out there. They get frustrated because they receive no income despite all of the work they have done. And that's totally understandable; we want to get returns on our time!

This book will streamline the process so you can go from start to finish on one thing, and get it out into the world so you can reap the rewards.

When starting with the one item, or minimum viable product, we are not solving every conceivable problem, but getting to the core need of the customer, then building on it based on what works and customer feedback.

Remember, even though creating something takes time, delaying your product out for six months to make it perfect may not serve your people; they have to wait for all that time (& may find someone else...) when your minimum viable product when could be helping them now!

Instead of solving Every Problem, solve the Most Important One

From Prototype to Production

After you have created your minimum viable product and you have people using it and loving what you're doing; you don't want to be a one hit wonder. You want to keep helping these people, right?

After the initial product is out in the world; we go back through all of your original ideas from your brain dump, and review what happened with your first idea. We can make sure the second one is not only as successful, but more successful and targeted to your audience.

There are a lot of different processes we can use, but first we need to see what worked and what didn't.

Were there any unintended outcomes, positive or negative? Did your course aimed at older women appeal more to a younger audience? Did you design an amazing shovel that more people are using as a lever or crow bar because the handle has amazing strength? We need to analyse our progress and keep building our businesses and audiences. We'll drill down into some of these methods later on.

Thomas Edison famously did thousands of experiments to create the light bulb. When he presented the light bulb to the world one of the reporters asked him if he felt like he failed all of those times it didn't work before he actually created it.

"No, no my dear friend," he said. "I found a thousand ways NOT to make a lightbulb."

Business owners need to be prepared they might not hit it big on their first idea. It is about constantly testing the market and analysing what is working and what isn't.

Very, very few people get it 'right' the first time, so it is okay to have an idea that doesn't quite hit the spot. So remember that there's a good chance your subsequent programs will be more successful than the first.

It is absolutely necessary to note that **success is not absolute**. That is, you don't either 100% fail or 100% succeed. There is a lot of wiggle room in between those two options! It is highly likely you will have some success, work on new ideas, and build from there. Success is also dependent on the individual; what you may deem as unsuccessful may be viewed as a success by another.

Prototyping your ideas is about taking your ideas, implementing them, scaling them, and leveraging them to where they need to go.

If you don't Overcome Roadblocks

Some people become like a mouse on a wheel; they keep going around and around and can't move forward. They may take a new idea, try the same thing, but there is always a piece of the puzzle that doesn't quite fit. If they don't take the time to see what is the root cause of that stumbling block, they get stuck again & again and their ideas never get realised. Many people can't see a way forward because they haven't examined the first step: overcoming roadblocks.

If you don't get the Minimum Viable Product right and don't have the right steps in place, you spend a lot of time, energy, and potentially money into developing something but never finishing it. It is like making the cake batter, but never putting it in the oven. You just have a hot mess of half-baked ideas. If people want to come and buy your thing, but you don't actually have a thing, you can get disappointed and start feeling like you're not good enough. It is not that; you just didn't have a process in place to get it finished.

Some people are running on a hamster wheel.

Going around and around,

but never getting anywhere.

If you don't get Prototype to Production right

Some people get stuck when it comes to scaling for a variety of reasons. It can be like a one hit wonder you put it out there with some success, then it stops. All that effort you put in stops and the work isn't reusable. It is like a single use plastic bag rather than having reusable cotton bag. We need to look at continually improving and changing it depending on the market and what we predict will be needed in the future.

Chapter Three

Overcoming Roadblocks

Imagine you are going meet a friend for dinner, you've just sat down at the table, and your friend is already there waiting. Before they have even said "Hello" they immediately say, "Oh, I don't really think you are dressed appropriately for this restaurant."

You mention you didn't get the memo or something like that, then pick up the menu. Then they say, "Did you actually do your hair? It is pretty frizzy and on your left side you've got a lock or two sticking out there."

You make some comment about the kids or something else going through your mind. You look at your friend and they say, "Oh and I'm pretty sure everyone else has noticed too. Maybe you shouldn't have come..."

Ummm... Would you actually want to have dinner with that friend? Subconsciously, this is how many of us speak to ourselves; we are always telling ourselves there is something wrong with us, this is why others don't want to do things with us, or why they will not want our products. If we talk to ourselves like this, we won't have the confidence to succeed.

There are three areas that regularly come up when people talk about why they haven't done something: capability, perfectionism & time.

The Capability Roadblock

When we question whether we can actually do this, even when we probably can. We say things like "I don't have a certificate in this" or "I don't have the skills to finish this project." Sometimes we even put in Roadblocks (such as study) in a sub-conscious way of delaying putting our ideas into action. Sometimes capability then spills into the next area of self-sabotage...

The Perfectionism Roadblock

When we believe everything we do has to be the best and have no flaws. One of the biggest reasons people don't finish anything is because they get to a point and remember they forgot to include something and everyone will miss out if it is not there. Or

The voice in your head, if brought to life, is not likely to be someone you'd want to hang out with

they look at a piece of art they did which they believe still needs a tiny tweak here or there... But if we look at it from a customer's point of view, they have no idea.

They don't have the same sense of "perfectionism" we do, they just see a beautiful piece of art someone has created. Whether that white line was supposed to go upwards or across that day doesn't matter to them because they are looking at the whole picture.

The Time Roadblock

We think we don't have enough time to complete the things we need to do to get our ideas out there. This is often not the case. What it generally means is this particular item is not our top priority. Therefore, we prioritise other things and give them time. If you want to prioritise something, you need to give it time.

Sometimes things happen like a family emergency where you need to get to the hospital. If you didn't finish your online course tonight, that's fine, go to the hospital; these things happen. Other times we might get to the end of the weekend and didn't get time to make an advertisement for our new workshop.

The reality is, that probably wasn't true. This truth is probably, "I'm scared to make that advertisement because that means people may sign up for my course," "I'm scared nobody will," or "I'm scared everybody will."

Fear of Success or Fear of Failure?

All these Roadblocks come down to basically two fears: a fear of success, or a fear of failure. The fear of success and the fear of failure is usually why we don't do things rather than because we don't have time or we don't feel capable or we don't believe our work is good enough.

What if someone puts a negative comment on Facebook? What if someone suggests I should have done it differently? Or something is missing?

What if I put all this effort in and nobody likes it? Or (even worse for some people!) what if I put it out there and everybody LOVES it???

And when it comes down to it... both these fears are a fear of change. Yes; there are going to be some changes when you run your own business & have the flexibility to choose how & when you work. There may be a few things you miss... But what about the benefits?? Don't let your mind talk you out of it before you've begun!

When we look at photographs of ourselves, the first thing we look for are our flaws. My nose is too big, my hair is too scruffy, or my chin is too low etc.... When other people look at your photos, they are not looking at the dimensions of your nose, chin, or scruffy hair, they see the vibrant inner beauty of this person they love, with a smiling face, interacting with others.

They look at your picture with a completely different lens. That is what many of us do with our businesses. We look for the things that aren't working or aren't perfect, but others, just like with the photograph, see the great work we are doing making a difference and being successful.

Overcoming Self-Sabotage

Firstly, when you are talking to yourself, you usually talk in absolutes. Yes or no. Truth or lie. Absolute success or utter failure. In reality, for almost everything there is space between black and white, there are many shades of grey in between.

For example, if you are saying "I don't have time" or "I have time to complete everything," you realise that every point away from "I don't have time" is closer to "I have completed everything." Then you can make lots of little steps and you are further away from your start point than when you started. We need to move away from absolutes to further down the continuum.

When you hear yourself say "I don't" in your head, remind yourself that is an absolute. It is generally not true. There is always in between.

Secondly, the reason a lot of these blocks are in place is because of things from the past. We are all different. Some have had traumatic things happen, but the memories don't have to be huge for them in impact us today. When we search back in our memories, they can be simple things that define our beliefs today.

I remember as a kid helping out on our farm. Sometimes it would be pouring rain, but the cows still had to be brought in. I remember the sound of rain on the thick farm rain coats, similar to that of a heavy storm on a tin roof. And remember feeling safe & dry even when the storms were there.

Still to this day, I love the sound of rain on a tin roof; and that may be just one of the reasons we bought the house we did!

Absolute Positives	Absolute Negatives
I don't have any money	I am insanely wealthy
I don't have any time	I have nothing to do with my time
I am dying	I never get sick
I don't know anything; I can't do anything at all.	I know everything; there's nothing more to learn!

Some of these memories, like the one I mentioned earlier about someone telling me to be quiet and let someone else had a turn, also stay with us. The teacher didn't mean forever, just for that moment, but in my heart it has stuck for years and years. Luckily there are some really cool techniques to help with these.

Removing Roadblocks From the Past

There are many ways you can move forward from blocks in the past. This is not my zone of genius, however here are a few ways that I have found helpful to move forward.

There are a variety of practitioners who can help with one on one sessions or in groups. Depending on your roadblock, you may want to seek outside help, especially if there's significant trauma.

One method I use is the **Aroma Freedom Technique**. With this technique, we don't have to relive our memories, we are not talking them out to everybody, we're just finding out why we might have an issue with, for example, advertising our work or going live on Facebook, or asking people to pay what we would like for something, which is a huge roadblock for some people.

With this technique, we can look at our memories, work out why they are there, and realise they are not serving us now. If they are deep seated it can take a number of sessions, but we can move those roadblocks over time. By looking at the memories & acknowledging their place; they don't need to hinder us again in the future.

The book **Feelings Buried Alive Never Die** by Karol K Truman is an amazing book, which looks at how our thoughts impact both our mental & physical health; and how to reprogram our subconscious so that we don't keep repeating negative beliefs that don't serve us anymore; beliefs like "I'm not worthy to receive income" or "My friends won't like me if I become successful".

There are so many thoughts that we constantly tell ourselves that simply aren't true, and not supporting us moving forward... so let's get rid of them!

The *awareness* of the issues is so important because once you recognise a roadblock and acknowledge it, palm it off and say, "You know what? I know why I feel this way or think this way, and that's just not true." You can use that mentality, acknowledge it and move on.

When you recognise a roadblock & acknowledge it, palm it off and move on.

If you are still feeling stuck and would like more help; check out my 5 day Stuck to Smashing It Challenge:

Releasing Perfectionism

When we start writing down our thoughts, we have all of this stuff we THINK we need to do. For example, if I'm going to make cupcakes for someone, I had better go out and do a decorating course because I want them to look good. I might need to buy a new cupcake tray & wrappers in her favourite colours. I might need to find a new recipe and ... and so on... It explodes into *project creep*.

You had this core idea and layered so much stuff onto it, it blew out of proportion: you got overwhelmed and thought you obviously couldn't go and create 1,000 cupcakes for someone's wedding so you can't make any cupcakes for a friend. Seems ridiculous... but we do it ALL THE TIME!!

Once we start looking at the "fluffy stuff" and realise it doesn't actually need to all be done, the project is much more achievable. The core idea is so much more achievable and we are more motivated to push the button and take a step forward.

It is all about focusing on just the necessary things. People often see the fluffy stuff as more exciting. They might get excited about designing the logo & flyers for their new business, and spend less time on creating the actual product (by the way; you DO need a logo etc. but it doesn't have to take weeks! Go back and look at perfectionism if you need to…).

So much of the time they allocate to their work goes to the fluffy stuff and not the necessary actions. The product never gets finished, you get disappointed, and the cycle goes on.

At least 80% of your time needs to be spent on the necessities; the actions that will get your product out to your customers & all the logistics around that.

But why not 100%?? (I know some of you are asking that!!) Because life is meant to be fun; and your business is no different. It is fun to spend some time on the Fluffy Stuff and doing random things; and so have fun!! Just make sure you know when you are working on Fluffy Stuff and that it doesn't take precedence over the necessary things!

Valuing Your Ideas

The 'Expert Dilemma' is when you have the skills that you don't value as much because they are natural for you.

When you know something, it becomes your normal, and because it is your normal, you don't value it as much. I grew up on a dairy farm, and one of my jobs was milking cows. From eight or nine years old I could milk cows. When you're milking cows, you also learn to identify red flags for their health too. We fed our cows hay so I drove a tractor, put out fences and all of these things were normal for me as a farm kid.

But for people who grew up in the city, that was not their normal, and just going near cows might possibly really freak them out! That's okay, that's not your normal or your zone of genius.

And on the flip side; not everyone has the same set of skills YOU have; I can honestly say, I do not have the same set of skills as you. There are things that you do much better than I.

Some people are completely in awe that I can drive a tractor. For me it is normal, I grew up doing it; just get in the tractor and do the things. But it's like learning to drive a car. Most adults can drive cars, but if you ask a 10-year-old to drive a car down a street, it may become a little interesting... It's just not their normal.

When we have these "normal" skills for us, we tend to undervalue them because it is quick & easy for us. You don't have to think about the tasks a lot of the time, it is automated in our mental processes. Something that might take us five minutes might take someone else an hour because they had to work out the individual steps.

When you think of costing that five minutes of my time, you tend to undervalue yourself. For someone else they might be grateful you saved them $100 because you did it and they didn't have to spend two hours trying to work it out.

This is the "Expert Dilemma".

Hobbies vs. Business

When people take a hobby and turn it into a business; they can struggle. When a hobby is a hobby, you are not expecting to make money out of it, there are no time constraints, you're having fun along the way, and it doesn't matter. If you have customers, they are usually friends so it doesn't matter if it takes a little longer, or the fabric is slightly different to the one they chose.

When that changes into a business, expectations change overnight. You go from, "I am just having fun and relaxing" to "I have to get this many widgets out the door exactly to spec with everything perfect."

Perfectionism comes back to bite us again. We need to make money because it is a business now. Neither one is right or wrong, but you need to know which camp you're in, so you know what your expectations are.

(Clarification: If you are reading this book to turn your ideas into business: then you MUST think about your ideas as business! Got it?)

Undervaluing Ourselves

When we undervalue ourselves, it creates resentment to what we are doing and we get disappointed in ourselves. We feel like we are doing so much and not getting enough back. This happens so often in start-up businesses.

New business owners think they need clients, they want to help so many people, but they're not experienced yet, so they can't charge a lot. This creates a dichotomy of "I'm doing so much but I'm not getting paid much... But I don't want to value myself too high because then my clients will go away." We have to work out the middle ground of how to value ourselves & our clients.

Women that are firstly marketing to their friends and family with 'mates' rates' can struggle to bridge the divide. We can have friends who are customers, but we have to treat them like a customer in that setting. You may give them a discount because you love them so much, but you need to be okay with that in your head as well.

This can be a huge grey area, particularly for network marketers, mums, and women in general, because we just chat and talk about everything, and quite often our friends do become our clients & vice versa.

You are in business now. What you sell has a market value and you can determine what that market value is. For most people it's difficult to put a high value on what they do because it is their new normal and they think it is not special. But for most purchases, clients would probably pay a higher price than what you think they would, if you communicate it right.

You are in business and you need to get paid for it. You have to cover your costs & feel valued in your business, so it is not just picking a number out of the air. Your prices do not need to be set in stone either; as you gain more experience and your business increases, your prices can change accordingly.

*It's your Choice.
Is this a Hobby or a
Business?*

During a court testimony in 1878, James McNeill Whistler was asked the very high price he had set for a piece of artwork he had created in just two days.

"Oh, two days! The labour of two days, then, is that for which you ask two hundred guineas!"

"No;—I ask it for the knowledge of a lifetime." [*A4]

[*A4] https://babel.hathitrust.org/cgi/pt?id=hvd.fl4mls&view=1up&seq=27

This historical account has then been cited as the basis of the 'Picasso Principle'; which comes from the story (it was hard to find out the exact details, so a folklore story it may stay!) of when Picasso was approached by a lady who recognized him.

"Maestro, I know your work. Could you do a drawing for me right now?" she asked.

"Certainly Ma'am," he said.

He spent two minutes and sketched the most beautiful drawing of her and handed it to her.

"Maestro! That is magnificent. What do I owe you?" she asked.

"That will be 200 francs," he replied.

"Oh my! That is such a lot of money. You only spent two minutes doing it!" she lamented.

"Madam, I spent two minutes doing it, and a lifetime to learn how to do it in two minutes, you're paying for a lifetime of experience."

The *Picasso Principle* outlines how we don't value the time we have taken to learn what others ask us to do.

This is absolutely the case with most of us. It may only take a few moments to do what you've done, but it has taken you a lifetime of experience; you've invested time, money and energy into creating not just a business, the skills you are marketing now. Once you recognise this, it should give a different perspective on how to price yourself.

There is no perfect price for your product. I can't tell you that you need to charge $X for your product or service, because they are all different & you live in different places (yes, that's definitely a factor!). Different products have different price points.

You need to make sure you are not feeling like you're being ripped off. You also need to make sure you don't feel like you are ripping your customers off either.

The upper end can feel very scary. You may think about the time you worked in a day job and were paid a certain amount, so that is what your time is worth. Just as with Picasso, that is not the case.

They gave those *jobs* a value (the actions you were performing), not you. When you work on that upper limit, I would encourage you to think about it being more than what you think it is right now.

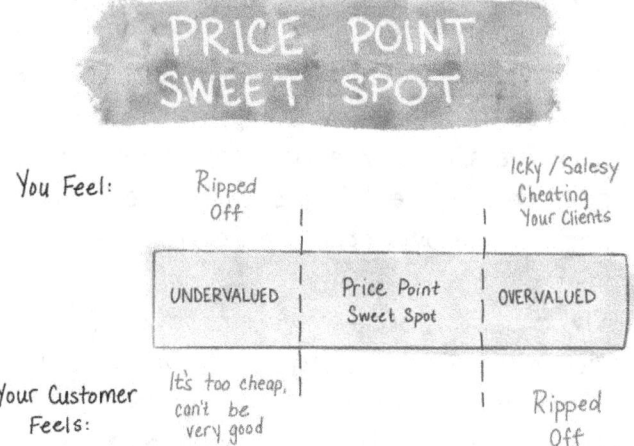

I ask for the knowledge of a lifetime

— James McNeill Whistler

People actually value your stuff when they pay for it. I used to run free workshops, workshops that cost $5, and workshops that cost $50+. For the ones people paid $50+, there were less people, but more engagement, and more people raving about them saying they got so much value.

For the $5 workshops, people came, people went; they were not changed in the way those that paid more were. For the free classes, it was 50:50 whether people would even show up! The engagement was low because they had no vested interest in it.

When things are cheap or free, people will not value them as much as you might want them to. When you price it appropriately, people will see it as an investment in time AND money, and will value your product more.

Wouldn't you prefer to have less people with a positive change, than many with little to no change?

Imagine you are at a barbeque and your stockbroker friend tells you about this really great stock that is going to go up in value they think you should go and look at as it will make you lots of money. You walk away thinking they are a good stockbroker, they are successful, and maybe you should listen to them, but in reality you are probably not going to do anything about it.

If you employ a stockbroker, pay them a commission, and they recommend the same stock, you are much more likely to invest because you are paying for that advice.

When you are paying, you are more likely to act than when it is just a suggestion from a friend. If your business is in a category where people ask you for advice or recommendations, and as a friend you tell them what you do, perhaps think about turning that into a paid relationship purely because the impact of your advice will be more valued in a professional situation.

Do you Give Away Free Stuff?

Free items are there, not to be your be all and end all, but to be a magnet for other purchases. There is no reason you can't give away things for free, you just need to make sure they are working for you to build rapport, get a purchase, repeat business, or referral.

There needs to be a purpose for that free stuff. If you are just giving away random stuff for free with no purpose, that's called a "present", not a business activity. You're going to feel like you give away a lot of money.

If the free items are to increase your audience or get repeat business, you can use it like an advertising budget.

People don't trade money for free stuff, but they do trade other things like time, attention, and their contact details. They can be valuable assets for your business. They may be paying in currencies other than money, but it is important those currencies are beneficial to your business.

For example, you may provide prospective customers with a free PDF on how to plant a tree correctly. If you are running a nursery that sells plants or a provider of gardening equipment, then showing that you have knowledge in this area, and your advice is good is reassuring to the customer and showing your authority.

In exchange for this free advice, they usually would provide you with their email address so you can contact them later down the track with other specials.

As many people are giving away free items, especially digital ones, you need to make sure that your audiences values your freebies enough to give you their details. In the digital world it is usually an email address & name.

Also, if you don't need a piece of personal data (i.e. phone number) to deliver the freebie; don't ask for it. If you ask for too much; people may just turn away.

Money is not the only currency of value. We also trade time, attention and permission to market to us.

Decision Time

You need to choose whether things are going to be free or paid.

You need to choose whether you have a hobby or a business.

You need to choose whether you are interacting as a friend or a business owner.

You are making decisions all the time, so **own those decisions.** Even if you make a "wrong" decision, allow yourself to take note & learn, just like Thomas Edison. Likewise, if something worked really well, note your actions so you can replicate it later.

Now that you've made the decision to turn your ideas into business; let's show you how!

Chapter Four

The 5 Steps

Turning Your Ideas into a Business

When I sit down and talk to people and they say they would love to build their own business, have their own craft shop, or teach people how to work with their hands, or about knowledge they have, it is always a pie in the sky. They always say, "Yeah, I would love to do this someday." They have no actual plan.

I ask questions like:

"What are you doing now to get there?"

"What is your first step?"

"Who's going to want your product (your target audience)?"

They look at me like I am asking them something in a foreign language. Many of them actually don't believe it could be a reality.

When I asked the questions, it was like taking their dreams and smashing them together with a big dose of practicality. And in their minds, there was no connection between the business dream and reality.

I realised there was a logical progression to these questions. Once you have answered one, you have discovered the first step. Then you could move on to the next one, and put a plan in place to go from dreaming about running your business, to actually having the steps in place to get it up and running.

We are engineering all the time whether we know it or not. We are creating solutions for things. We are always trying to do something a little better; many of us just don't realise it. The five steps is about optimising the process for taking your ideas and turning them into a reality.

If you take the journey one step at a time, it doesn't matter whether you are an engineer, or what kind of person you are, everyone can turn their idea into a business.

If you are in a dark room, you can still do things, but it will take you a long time. You can still find things, feel your way around them, pick up things, probably achieve something, but it is not going to be fun, or quick. It takes more time and energy. This 5 step process is turning on that light and giving you the opportunity to see step by step the process of getting to and realising your business. These steps are your light bulb.

Step 1: The Brain Dump

When kids get excited, they have a million and one ideas, often can't get their words out, and their hands go everywhere. Try and get a five year old to tell you the best thing that has just happened. Maybe it is their birthday and they just got THE BEST PRESENT EVER (you know that's how they would say it!!)... Watch; they just can't get all the words out, no sentence is finished and you probably know the colour, the size and how it sounds (and that IT'S AWESOME!!)... Their brain is moving at 100 miles an hour and their mouth just can't keep up!

When we have business ideas it is exactly the same. We often have all of these thoughts that cascade all at once. If we don't get them down on paper, they get lost. You remember the feeling when you had all of these ideas, but the actual details of them can be lost. It's like you remember that you *did* have a dream and whether it was pleasant or not... but recalling the details is near impossible.

If you are in a dark room, you can still get things done. But it's going to be a lot easier with the lights on!

When writing down our thoughts; we don't want to cull them in any way. We don't want to think "this one is bad" or "this one is better" just get them all out.

Neither does it have to be neat or tidy. Make it colourful! You can use coloured markers if you like rainbows, that's all good. There may even be added creative bonuses from using different colours. Feel free to draw your ideas if that resonates better with you too.

When we have done the brain dump, remember they are not all necessarily going to come to fruition and they don't all need to be addressed right now; and that is okay. It is okay to have an idea that is not for you, or you are not going to do right now.

If you have a lot of thoughts and you are not 100% sure where you want to put your time and energy, quickly skip forward to the chapter on *Value and Time Spent* and come back to this (this is the only time I'm going to tell you to skip ahead!).

We are not going to stress about whether we think we can achieve them or whether people will like them, we are just putting our dreams and goals down on paper with no filters.

Once you have everything on paper, you can take a breath. It is so satisfying when something is done and you get to tick it off. There are a few interesting things that happen when you have things down on paper or post-it notes.

You *free up real estate* in your head. When you have all these thoughts you are hanging on to, you don't have the same capacity to think about other things because you are trying so hard to remember those thoughts. You know they are important and you know there is value there.

Once you have them on paper, you can *look at them as a whole*. When they are thoughts in your head, you cycle through them. You think about one thing, then another, then another... oh you forgot about that one, so have to go back.

You don't have the big picture process in place. You might realise that two thoughts you thought were totally unrelated, can link up with this beautiful yellow highlighter, and realise their connection now that you can see the big picture.

You can do a brain dump anytime that suits you. My favourite place, and when my thoughts are most active, is in the shower (I have a waterproof notepad in the shower with a pencil so I don't lose those thoughts!).

A brain dump could be as simple as a five minute exercise, or you could sit down with a cup of tea and relax in your favourite chair and spend half an hour. It doesn't have to be a long amount of time. If you have a thought, I encourage you to put it on a post-it, even if you are cooking dinner; get it down.

I was coming home from grocery shopping in the car and thought of something I needed to write down. I pulled over to the side of the road; I didn't have a journal or notebook or anything useful with me, argh!

My girls asked what I was doing because they wanted to get home. I ended up scribbling my ideas on the back of the grocery receipt; which ended up being a workshop and how this book came into fruition.

Your Product Solar System

As you work through your brain dump; you'll likely find that there is something, a theme or concept, that you have passion & skill in and ties together a lot of your ideas. This theme or concept is your "Sun".

You know how a solar system works; you have the Sun in the middle; and around the Sun, there's planets that orbit. And then around each of the planets, there are satellites (moons) that orbit them. You can think about your business in this way.

The Sun is your central theme; your passion, your focus that all the products that you develop revolve around; they relate to the Sun in some sort of way.

The planets are your major, marketable products. These are actual products that people can purchase. It may be a physical product, digital media or coaching/labour services. Your planets are all distinct; they all relate to the Sun, but not necessarily to each other directly.

Then each planet may have a number of satellites. These products are like accessories to the planets; they complement and build on the concept on the planet it revolves around.

For example, you might have a course that teaches people how to use woodworking tools. A satellite for this course might be an eBook (or physical book) with the plans on how to make specific wooden products using the tools and skills they have learnt about in the course.

If you would like a step by step guide on how to create your own product solar system, please check out my Little Ideas, Big Business workbook:

Once you have your first product solar system (yes, it's always a work in progress!), you'll see that there's a LOT going on. So how do we work out where to start?

Step 2: Figure Out & Focus on One Idea

Figuring out your first project or idea to focus on can be a stumbling block for many people. Once we can focus on one, we can make sure we get all the steps in place to get that finished and actually achieve something.

One of the roadblocks for some people is they get halfway through their project or idea, then change ideas, or want to get three projects up and running. They spread themselves too thin to get anything finished.

So we choose one idea and one project.

It has to be something you love. You are doing this business and you need to have a passion for it. You want to be able to enjoy what you are doing and work towards something you love, so you can serve your people better, and they can go on and serve other people. You might currently have a job you don't like; don't jump from one dud job to another!

Look at your ideas and see if any of them form a cluster that can be grouped together, then choose one from this list. The other ideas can come later (we will talk about second and third idea integration later in the book). The second and third ideas will naturally come out later & can build on the efforts you put into the first.

Money Now vs Half-Baked vs Concept Ideas

When looking at which of your ideas to move forward with, it can be tricky to work out which one to focus on! I like to categorise them into three types.

Money Now Ideas

Money now ideas are the ones where everything is there and you just need to do a few tweaks and advertise or market it to your class, clients, or the world. Usually this is something you've been doing with people informally or as a hobby and you just need to formalise your work. This is a great place to start; however can also be a trap.

Remember we talked about how we want to make sure you're passionate about your work and love what you do? Sometimes people fall into the trap of "other people say I am good at this so I should make it my work/business".

If that was true; I could be doing anything from making macramé hanging pots to milking cows…

MONEY NOW	HALF-BAKED	CONCEPT
• Ready to go	• You know the process to get it done	• Pie in the Sky ideas
• Great for immediate cash		• Big Dreams... but no clue how to implement
• Opportunity to get to market fast	• Needs work to implement	• Can be daunting due to size and scale
• May not be in your Zone of Genius	• May require investment or capital than 'Money Now' does	• Big Ideas
• Can be easy to follow distractions	• Can drain your time if 5 steps not followed	• Amazing Opportunities when in your Zone of Genius
	• May not be in your Zone of expertise	• Requires Long-term vision, planning, and commitment

And while it's true that I have made some cash from doing both those things; it's not my ultimate passion nor something I believe will utilise my expertise to its fullest. There are people whose passion for these things is much greater than mine, and I am happy for them to pursue careers there.

And you may find the same thing; there may be multiple things you CAN do... but what is your passion?

When looking at money now ideas; some may literally be a temporary thing to make money now, so that you can pursue the bigger thing afterwards. They may be steppingstones to allow you to them realise your big idea. If so; treat them as such and don't lose sight of that bigger idea!

Half-Baked Ideas

Half-baked ideas are where you kind of know the process, but haven't done a lot of the actual work there, so there is some time & energy involved in getting it up and running. Perhaps you want to ramp up a hobby you have; you know what you need to do it on a small scale, but moving into production stage would require some more equipment etc.

Your half-baked ideas may end up being the "workhorse" of your income down the track; larger, regularly-selling products that you can rely on. Just remember: to be an income stream, they need to be *finished*. The time & effort needs to be put in to get these ideas to market, so they can be that income stream for you.

Concept Ideas

Concept ideas are the ones you wish you could do one day. Those big dreams that may seem, at the moment, far from reality and disconnected from the now. *Don't discard these* because some are the most brilliant ideas you will ever have!

Maybe there are some money now or half-baked ideas that are stepping stones to your big idea... Maybe you can start saving for capital or talking to people about how to make it happen.

If the big idea is something you think about often; you'll find it comes out in conversations and your subconscious is taking its own steps to start putting the wheels in motion.

But we also need to think about income we can get now. If you have money-now ideas which you can give yourself a deadline of a week or two to get out there, you get satisfaction of having work done and putting more time into concept ideas for the future. Use the previous table to categorise where your ideas fit into your business.

So, how ready are you to put any of your ideas into action? If you have three ideas, are any of them more "half-baked" than the others?

Is there one that is almost ready to go now and there are just a few little steps to go? They are the kinds of ideas you may want to focus on first rather than a concept in the sky you are not sure how to proceed with.

Get some smaller wins under your belt before tackling the big concept ideas!

Step 3: Putting in Celebration Dates (Deadlines)

The word deadline can produce a level of fear and an actual physiological reaction when some people hear it. If you don't like the word deadline, call it a celebration date, or achievement date. This is a day you are *looking forward to*. That may sound like a foreign concept, if you've lived in fear of deadlines all your life!

The big deadline is your achievement day; where you are ready to share your product with the world. We shouldn't be scared of that, it should be celebrated!

The word 'deadline' strikes fear into many hearts. What if we change it to something more inspiring?

Our bodies need an amount of stress to survive. Athletes will not get their bodies to peak performance without some level of stress in their training. On race days, the adrenaline rush gives them more to give in the race. We actually achieve better under a certain amount of stress.

What can happen though, is if the stress levels are too high and you don't feel you have enough time to achieve what you want to achieve; it can hamper rather than help.

But if there is not enough stress, it is easy for people to keep putting things off until tomorrow, and there are a million tomorrows coming where nothing will get done.

'Whelm' is the amount of force to create change. Imagine you are standing and someone comes and pushes you as hard as they can in the back and you fall flat on your face. Cue "overwhelm".

Imagine instead, they came and very gently touch your back and nothing happens; there's no movement. Cue "underwhelm".

But if someone comes and uses just enough force on your back, you will be able to walk forwards and make progress. Bingo. The aim is achieved and it doesn't take forever. Just the right amount of whelm!

Whelm is all about making sure the amount of force is at an appropriate level. Think about a school or university assignment that has a deadline of 5.00pm Friday. You have to click the submit button at 4.59pm.

How much work do you do in the three weeks beforehand? How much do you do a week out? How much do you do on the day it is due?

How much do you do in the hour before you have to push that submit button...?

Having a deadline and knowing it has to be finished is very motivating. If we don't have a deadline we feel is close enough, we won't take the steps towards achieving that goal.

For example, would you start saving now for a large international holiday you want to take in 5-10 years, or "when the kids get to high school"? Or does it seem too far away to put the cash away for? The deadline might be just too far away for us to be able to visualize & actually take action towards.

For this reason, it is great to put in celebration dates (deadlines) in along the way, so that you can keep the whelm at a level that maximizes your progress.

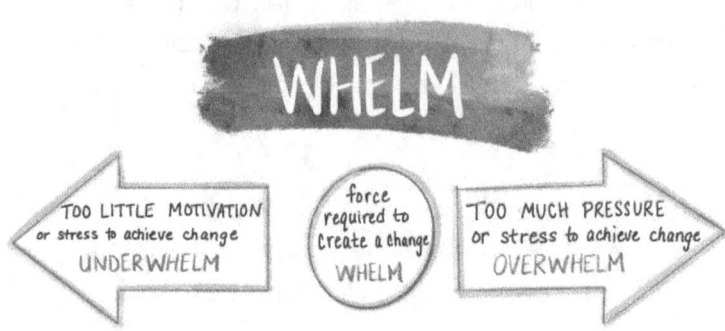

Some people don't have a deadline because they have no idea about the actions involved. We have to work out what actions are involved so the work can get done. Other people don't have a deadline because they are worried about not achieving it. There is fear of failure and fear of success. If you don't have a deadline, ask yourself why not and have a look at some of those roadblocks to see if any of them are coming in to play.

Step 9: The Minimum Viable Product

When software was first developed, they believed the best program had to have all the bells and whistles and every single thing done. It might take a couple of years, maybe three or more to develop this all-encompassing piece of software.

When they released it, they realised most people used only a tiny portion of it and they could have released those parts years ago.

Fast forward 10 – 15 years and now we see a new app comes out, then a month later there are new features released. Instead of putting on all the bells and whistles to begin with, they put out what is needed by their market at the time, so they can get it out to people and produce an income. They then make changes and upgrades later on.

Sometimes they get it wrong; we've all seen it! There are bugs and glitches everywhere; then they do an update (using this valuable user feedback!) and when it's fixed, you have a product that works; usually with even more features than the original. The beauty of the digital world!

When we are talking about getting your *minimum viable product* (MVP) out there so you can start making an income sooner, there's a few things we need to remember:

We need to *ditch perfection*. This comes back to one of those roadblocks. It is really difficult for some people who want the best and only the best for their product.

Whether it is absolutely perfect the first time or not, your customers need your product. Most of the time you're doing this because you've seen a need; so they need it now. They need it sooner than five years when you have decided it is perfect. Even in five years you will still probably decide it is not perfect and you still be creating on this wheel.

Having your product out there is more helpful than a perfect product in 10 years. The minimum is not worthless, it is worth much more than an unfinished 'perfect' product, because people can actually use it.

What is your product designed to do? What do your customers actually need your product to do for them? For example, if you are designing a new shovel, it needs to dig holes. It doesn't need *all* the features; like smashing rocks or having stamped on embellishments. It needs to do its primary function; dig holes.

Remember, you can always add features later. It needs to do the core thing first. We need to focus on that. Look at necessities vs. niceties (we'll come back to this later).

Once your product is out there it means you are producing income, and people are enjoying the benefit from your product. You are also getting your name out there so people know where to go when they need something extra in that same space.

The minimum is not worthless at all; it's worth much more than an unfinished perfect product.

The minimum viable product is not really about focusing on the least, but focusing down on the most important element or the thing people absolutely need done with your product. Eventually you will create more, so this is giving you the space to actually have something out there and build on it later.

When you ask a kid what their dream house is, it will have a waterslide, a jumping castle, possibly even a zoo, and campfire in the backyard. Will it have a kitchen, a bathroom or a bed? Well, maybe a bed so the stuffed toys can rest...

When we think about our dreams, we can think about all of the glitzy stuff, and sometimes what it is actually supposed to do gets lost in the fog. We really want to make sure the minimum viable product does what it says to do first.

Every house needs a bathroom.

Step 5: Prioritise Your Actions

We now have our idea, we have chosen our minimum viable product, now it is time to work on our action plan.

If you look at your ideas, and your brain dump of actions you have written to get this task done; it may seems overwhelming; so I like to prioritise & categorise the actions, or tasks, on the table.

Necessities, Niceties & Bonuses

First we want to break down our minimum viable product into necessities, niceties and bonuses.

Necessities are the things that really, *really* need to be done. If you do not do them, you cannot have a product, or you cannot get your product out there.

Advertising and marketing (in some way) are essential to get your product out there. Some people don't like it, but they are necessary because no one will buy your product if they don't know it exists.

There are other things that are needed. You may have to buy materials to physically make something. You may have to develop a website if you are delivering something online. These are the necessities to have a product at the end of it. They may not be glamourous; but don't ignore them!

The things that are nice to have, our *niceties*, might still relate to that core idea, but are not actually necessary for that core idea to function. For example, if you are shipping out a product, you might have personalised packaging.

It is very nice, promotes your brand and goes with the item, but is it actually necessary? Will you end up spending more time on the personalised packaging than producing the thing itself...?

Bonuses are things the customers are probably going to like, but have nothing to do with your core idea. If we take a look at the shovel again, a bonus might be they get a rake to go with it. It doesn't have anything to do with the shovel, but they might be interested in it too because they are an avid gardener, and hence are buying your awesome shovel.

People love talking about the nicety stuff, like making their packaging pretty and having their initials over the wrapping paper. They love talking about the bonuses for clients because they want to give them more value.

Sometimes the necessities get lost because no one wants to talk about how to market their product, or developing their website in the platform they will use to sell their product. We need to make sure the necessities have the time and headspace required before we move on to the nice stuff.

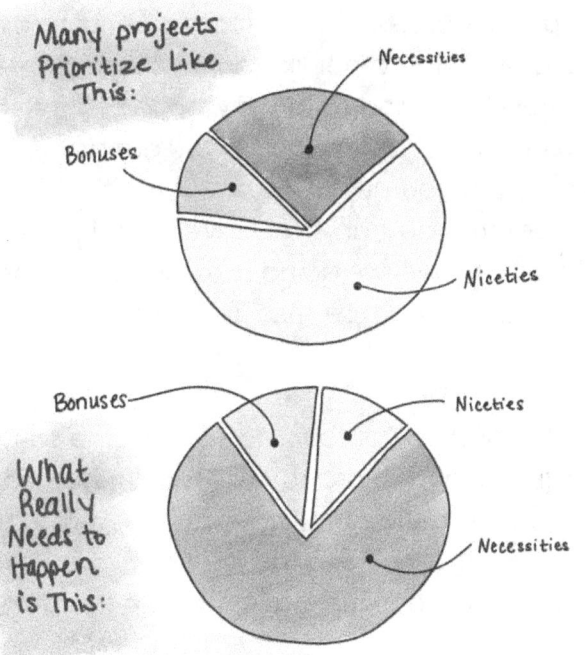

Series & Parallel Actions

Once we have worked out what the necessities, niceties and bonuses are, we need to work out how to implement them. Because I am a solar power engineer, I look at this process like an electrical circuit. (Please, let me nerd out just a little here!)

Some things are connected in a series. They are connected one after the other like a list with step one, step two, step three and so on. If you don't do step three, you can't get to step four. If you are doing an online workshop, you need to know the title of the workshop before you can start advertising it. If we just put it out there we are doing an online workshop; no one will come because they don't know what it is about.

Some are parallel, so you can do them at the same time and they don't interact with each other. For our workshop example, once we have the title and online bookings set up, we can do the PowerPoint presentation and continue advertising at the same time.

Parallel things are things that need to be done, but are not dependent on each other.

And of course; you'll likely find that your implementation steps are a beautiful mix of series & parallel actions.

Series or Parallel Tasks

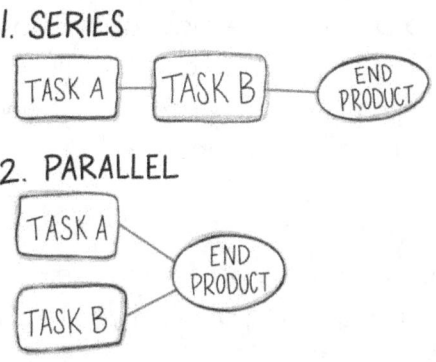

The Combined Workflow Model
Series + Parallel

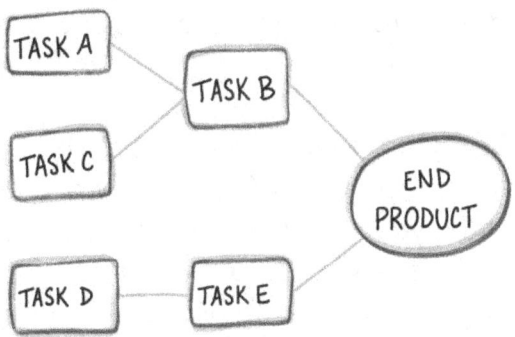

PUTTING IT ALL TOGETHER: TASK A & C NEED TO BE DONE BEFORE TASK B. TASK D NEEDS TO BE DONE BEFORE TASK E; AND NEITHER OF THOSE TASKS RELY ON THE STATUS OF TASK A, B OR C.

Identifying the necessities can be difficult in terms of actually knowing what needs to be done from a technical point of view as well as a business point of view. For example, if you're a craftsperson, you know how to paint, make clay, or do mosaics. But turning that into a workshop and knowing how to do it yourself at home, to then working out how to teach it, making sure you have enough materials and so on, can be challenging.

I highly recommend seeing if there are others doing similar things and looking at what you really need to do or not do.

Sometimes people struggle to accept niceties or bonuses even exist; they see it ALL as necessities. When we have this brilliant idea, we think everything needs to be done because it is so brilliant. It doesn't need to be bigger than Ben-Hur. Allowing yourself to acknowledge there are in fact niceties and bonuses is key.

If you are doing that mosaic workshop and you have the materials for each person and their work stations all set up, then you think you have to find a buffet lunch because the workshop ends at lunchtime... that is not a necessity. It is a nice thing to do and more likely a bonus for your workshop, but it is not necessary.

A Note on Distractions

Distractions come in many forms, and some of them can actually be in the form of our ideas. If you have an idea that kind of "has to be done" and you think you "would like to do it", what you really might be doing in your head is thinking, "If I work on this, I don't have to do my big thing". I don't have to work at my passion or the thing that going to take a bit longer and more effort, I'm going to do all these tiny projects and skirt around the edges and never really do my big thing.

Check out the section on Roadblocks... You might recognise this one as being the fear of success or fear of failure.

Acknowledge these little projects as distractions which are not helping you achieve what you want in the long-term, cross it off your brain dump, say goodbye, and move on. It might sound a little harsh, but trust me; as one who has done a *lot* of tiny projects and spent literally YEARS jumping from tiny project to small job; it's not satisfying, it doesn't bring you joy and you feel like you are just pottering and wasting time.

There comes a time when you need a little more whelm to get you going.

Procrastination Habits

Along with distracting projects; you may be able to relate to this: habitual procrastination.

For me; an example of this is making a cup of tea. I really do enjoy a good cup of rooibos!

But when I notice that this is my 3rd or 4th cup of tea before lunchtime; I know that I'm actually procrastinating.

I am doing something that is not 'wrong' or 'bad'; and in that way justifying putting of whatever I have to do, until I have completed this small, unimportant, and ultimately meaningless in the scheme of things, task.

And then I'll probably find another...

Procrastinating usually is a sign of overwhelm; you feel you have to do or be too much right now, and so your brain (and productivity) just stalls completely.

Once we uncover & acknowledge this habit; we can, just like a roadblock, be aware of it, deal with it and move forward.

Have you got a procrastination habit?

Chapter Five

Prototype to Production

Once we have a working product it's time to optimise your product or service and make it better. Or roll out the next idea that complements your first idea. This requires analysing what happened with your minimum viable product prototype and incorporating that feedback into where you go next.

Usually we don't have one idea, but have multiple ideas as we saw in our brain dump, and as time goes on we want to refresh it. There might be new technology better suited to what you are doing, or you get feedback from your customers who suggest adding a new feature or taking a feature off to make it better for the next customers. They are generally not saying you did poorly, they are tips to serve your customers better or get your product out to more people.

When we have our prototype or our minimum viable product done, we can then look into our next ideas. Firstly, we must look at how our first product performed. We should get feedback so we can learn from it. Then we can create either version 2.0 or work on a slightly different idea.

Very few businesses are successful with their first product or idea, so if you are reading this part and feel like you fell flat with your prototype, you are not alone! It's okay and we are going to move forward and look at some reasons why.

You are embarking on a journey that few people take, and it can seem like you are alone in your roadblocks. Let me remind you that you aren't. Many have gone before you and the great thing about that, is that we can learn from their lessons and success.

For those who are numbers-people (my hand is UP!)... Here's some interesting stats on why small businesses fail.

Why am I telling you how your business can fail? Well, if you don't know what *could* be an issue for you... how can you prepare for it? Take a look at these causes, and make sure you have included strategies in your business to NOT be caught out.

The top 10 causes of small business failure

1. No market need: 42 %;
2. Ran out of cash: 29 %;
3. Not the right team: 23 %;
4. Got outcompeted: 19 %;
5. Pricing / Cost issues: 18 %;
6. User un-friendly product: 17 %;
7. Product without a business model: 17%;
8. Poor marketing: 14 %;
9. Ignore customers: 14 %; and
10. Product mistimed: 13 %.

Source - https://smallbiztrends.com/2019/03

Reflecting on Where You are Right Now

If you've already launched a product and you are reading this to improve your skills for the next one, it's a really good time to reflect on where you are right now.

Did you sell more or not as much product than expected?
Do you have feedback from your customers? And what did it say?
Did you use a survey, word of mouth, or social media?

Note that with social media, *many* more people will write a note if they are unhappy with something than if they are happy. If you don't have a lot of good comments, that doesn't mean there are not happy people out there, they may just not be as passionate to share this with you.

Were there any unintended outcomes?
For example, you created your product to do a particular thing, but you got feedback it was useful elsewhere. A large company produced a toothpaste that many people use as a deodorant too (bizarre I know, but it works!). They are now looking at ways to develop that product further, as they can see the benefits it has in other areas.

Have a look at your processes for identifying necessities.

Was there something you missed? Or was there something you were not aware you needed to do?
I have done many projects that I look back on, and reflect on the knowledge that would have been good to know.

It is useful to look back with curiousity, rather than regret, so that you can be in the right frame of mind to take away the lessons you learnt.

Same with your roadblocks, there's value insight to be learnt.

Did you not do something because you were scared your family and friends would not like what you're putting on social media? Did you try to achieve perfection & delay too long?
Again, look back with curiousity and reflection, rather than criticism & regret. You did what you did with the knowledge you had; and now you know more, so you can improve!

What are you going to celebrate?
And this is SO important. Don't look back and see just the things to improve; have a look at what you achieved! What you did really well; note these things down too, so that you can repeat them and give your customers an amazing experience!

Version 2.0 & Beyond

Iteration is the process of developing your idea. You'll recognize the use of that word in big business, or software companies. It's time to it to use in your enterprise. Start by asking a series of questions designed to reveal the strengths, weaknesses and opportunities that are available...

- Would you do what you did again?
- Does it need tweaking?
- Does it need changing in some way to make it more successful?
- Does the same thing need a different format?
- Did you do it online, but it would be better face to face?
- Would it be better as a weekly course rather than a workshop?
- What do you have to offer your clients now?
- Where is the best place for them to work with you next?
- Did it work for you?
- Did it work for your customers?
- Did it run so smoothly you are so happy with it, you could do it every weekend for the rest of your life?
- Did you go overtime?
- Was there not enough content for the time?
- Were there little things that needed changing?

- Did they want printed handouts rather than sending them a link?
- Did the clients want access to the information afterwards creating an opportunity for online course content so they can access this information all the time?
- Where do your clients go from here?
- What feedback did your customers give you? Can you provide that?
- Can they bring their friends along?
- Will they join you again if you do put something else out?
- How did we reach our first audience?
- Did we only advertise on Facebook, or the local community noticeboard?
- When we offered that product, did we only do it locally, so is there an area slightly further away we could try it?
- Is there a different social media platform you could use to create a larger or slightly different target audience?

When we start asking these questions, we can see some different next projects.

Perhaps your first audience targeted mums with younger kids. Could you tweak it slightly for mums with older kids who have left home? Or men with kids? Can you tweak it slightly to make it appealing to a slightly different audience?

Say you are in a florist business and you teach people to create floral arrangements, but your next idea is to teach people to install guttering on their house. It is unlikely to be the same audience. It is possible, but improbable.

The idea of teaching people to grow their own flowers fits more into your current business. You have a warm target market already there for your new idea as repeat customers.

If you built rapport and they loved what you did, they are likely to repeat with you. You are not starting from ground zero with those people.

Scaling the Business

Once your first idea is up and running, you go back to your brain dump. Maybe you have another 10 ideas! As you are unlikely to get through all of your ideas before new ones pop up, we need to look at where your time is best spent. We are not just looking at a dollar per hour value; there are a lot of things that have value.

For example, time versus money.

If you run a workshop or an event on a single day, you have put in effort up to that point with advertising, buying materials, developing content and worksheets, and so on. Once that event is over, if you have nothing else to offer your clients, it is single use effort. That time you spent on them is now over.

Let's then look at an online course; you spent time making videos & course content and put it all online. Once that is done, people can buy that course now AND into the future. The effort you put in at the start may be a little more as you had to work out how to create a website and do videos and so on, but that effort is more evergreen.

You will likely make changes along the way, but a big chunk of time you put into it is still valid three months, six months, even 12 months down the track. You can still get paid income for that online course well after the effort is put in.

NOTE: you will still need to put effort in to continue to reach your target audience & keep your info current.

That doesn't mean you should never do workshops again. You can remind people that if they loved this workshop, this is online course is how they can take it to the next level, or offer them more of your time, or a book. You can use that event to encourage those customers come back again.

Do a good job at your workshop and your customers are actually *paying you* to let them know about your other offers.

As you scale your business, time becomes a very real limiting factor. Here's some questions to help you scale up:

- Can you engage with more people at one time? (i.e. larger groups, online sessions etc.)
- Can you hire out tasks that aren't in your zone? (i.e. accounting, printing, graphic design, shipping)
- What are the tasks you MUST do? i.e. what tasks are you unwilling to hire out?
- What evergreen products are you able to produce?
- Is larger scale manufacturing an option for your products?
- How could you utilize digital automation? (i.e. scheduling social media, emails etc.)
- Do you want to have employees/contractors?
- What boundaries do you need to set, so that you don't become a slave to your business?

Some of these questions have definite answers; others will be good to ponder on as your business grows.

Your answers may change over time as well!

Chapter Six

It's Your Turn

This book is all about helping you earn more money in a way that really suits you, gives you more control, meaning, and flexibility. When people can have more time, money and flexibility, it has an enormous positive impact on their lives. This is about giving structure and focus on how to turn your ideas into a practical business that gives you the life you always dreamed of.

Your ideas are valuable. Use them wisely and take them seriously. I hope this book has a positive and profound impact on you, your family, and community.

Billy runs online and in person workshops, as well as personalized & group coaching to support her clients to turn their ideas into business. She also provides life coaching and a variety of online courses.

Billy loves to work with people who are ready to live the life they dream of and turn their ideas into amazing businesses.

For full details:

www.billymclean.com

www.ingramcontent.com/pod-product-compliance
Lightning Source LLC
Chambersburg PA
CBHW072015290426
44109CB00018B/2245